the **Beagle**

Buying, nutrition, care, behavior, health, reproduction and lots more

Contents

Foreword

The book you are holding is not intended to be a
complete "owners manual" for the Beagle. If we had
tried to cover all the information possible about this
breed, its history and development, feeding, training,
health, ailments and whatever more, this would be a
book of at least 500 pages.

What we have done however, is to collect basic
information to help the (future) owner of a Beagle
look after his or her pet responsibly. Too many people
still buy a pet before really understanding what
they're about to get into.

This book goes into the broad history of the Beagle,
the breed standard and some pros and cons of
buying a Beagle. You will also find essential
information on feeding, initial training and an
introduction into reproduction. Finally we give
attention to (day-to-day) care, health and some breed-
specific ailments.

Based on this information, you can buy a Beagle,
having thought it through carefully, and keep it as a
pet in a responsible manner. Our advice, though, is
not just to leave it to this small book. A properly
brought-up and well-trained dog is more than just a
dog. Invest a little extra in a puppy training course or
an obedience course. There are also excellent books
available that go deeper into certain aspects than is
possible here.

The About Pets Team

ibooks

A Publication of ibooks, inc.

An ibooks, inc. Book

ibooks, inc.

24 West 25th Street

New York, NY 10010

The ibooks World Wide Web Site

Address is:

http://www.ibooks.net

ISBN 0-7434-4540-6

First ibooks, inc. printing

January 2003

10 9 8 7 6 5 4 3 2 1

Cover photograph copyright © 2002

Cover design by j. vita

As the purchaser of this book, you are
entitled to access a free electronic book
version of the title for use with
Windows, Macintosh and Palm
computers and PDAs. To access the
"ebook" version, you may log onto
www.ibooks.net, click the "About Pets"
button and follow the directions.

Original title: *de Beagle*

© 1999 - 2002 Welzo Media Productions bv,

Warffum, the Netherlands

http://www.overdieren.nl

Photos:

Anne-marie Schuurman

en andere leden van

de Beagle Club Nederland

en Rob Doolaard

Printed in China

In general

The Beagle is a very old breed, so there have been a lot of people around the world before you that have owned one or more beagles. But one still often hears that Beagles are impossible, pigheaded little wreckers and can't be taught a thing. Nothing is further from the truth!

The Beagle is an independent dog with a strong will and its own opinion about things. As its master or mistress, you have to be able to, and want to, deal with this. If you respect your Beagle, your Beagle will respect you. You won't get respect just like that, but you will have to earn it. Bringing up a Beagle follows the same rules as bringing up a child. Calm, but consistent enforcement of law and order where necessary.

The history of the Beagle

Even before the birth of Christ, man used small dogs to hunt hares in packs. However, from the rare descriptions in ancient literature, these dogs did not appear to be like the Beagle as we know it today. Arrianus (approx. 95–175 BC) very precisely describes ancient Greek harrier dogs, that were very probably today's Beagle, especially with their unusual bark and their small body. There have been dogs of the Beagle type in the British islands for centuries. In his book written in 1879 under the pseudonym "Stonehenge," J.H. Walsh wrote, "A real Beagle is a miniature form of the Southern Hound." The Southern Hound is a variety of Foxhound. As far as we know today, the name Beagle came from "beag," "beg" or "beigh," Celtic for "small." The name "Beagle" was first used during the reign of King Henry VII between 1457 and 1509. In the private accounts of Henry VIII (1509-1547) there is a payment recorded to the "Beagle keeper," Robert Shere. From all these ancient documents, it appears that British nobility used the Beagle in packs to hunt hares. British nobility still does that today.

The Beagle arrived in America at the end of the 19th century, and Americans started to breed them, too. That's why we can measure the Beagle against two standards. These are the American and the British standards, of which more later. After the Second World War, British breeders crossed American and English Beagles, which substantially improved the breed.

Because the Beagle was primarily used to hunt small game, it belongs to the "Hounds" group. Other breeds in this group include the Basset Hound, the Afghan Hound, the Basenji, the Greyhound, the Harrier, and the Fox Hound. These dogs pursue game and track it by its scent.

In the past, there was almost no difference between the hunting Beagle and the show Beagle. Nowadays, there is a big difference between the two. The show dog is usually more compact and often smaller in build. The Beagle used for hunting is a somewhat larger Beagle with longer legs enabling it to move faster across plowed land and through bushes. More and more Beagles are now kept as show dogs and pets.

The Beagle and hunting
Since ancient times, the Beagle

has been used as a hunting dog working in packs, especially in Britain. It was also known under the name of "Small Coursing Dog." It was used for hunting hares and rabbits in packs. The Harrier and Foxhound are larger than the Beagle. Outwardly, the Beagle most closely resembles the Foxhound. Its head gives a soft impression, while the Harrier has a tough impression. The Beagle was always bred to drive game in a wide arch towards the huntsman, without human help, or in the case of a fox to drive it into its hole. This has produced its independent nature, which some people wrongly regard as pigheadedness.

Beagling, as the British call hunting with beagles, is done using a pack of 20 to 25 dogs. Their master selects the dogs to form the pack on the day of the hunt. The selection depends on the terrain on which the hunt will take place. The master first picks the lead dog, followed by the flanking dogs and then completes the pack with younger, less experienced dogs.

The pack scours the terrain. The master walks behind the pack and is assisted by helpers, the so-called whippers-in. These helpers ensure that the Beagles don't stray from the pack. A crack of the whip is enough to call the dogs to order without actually

hitting them. When one dog finds the scent it "cries." The lead dog checks the scent and then goes in full chase following it. The pack then follows the lead dog in "full cry." The master, the whippers-in and any spectators then follow at full-speed on foot, and they all need to be extremely fit! The legs of a Beagle in full sprint never seem to touch the ground. They develop high speeds, otherwise they would never be able to "catch" a healthy hare or fox.

The whippers-in fan out into a semi-circle to check the flanks of the pack. The twists and turns of the fleeing hare trying to shake off its pursuers are picked up by the flank dogs. These "warn" the lead dog, which immediately brings the pack back into line.

A healthy hare is faster than a chasing pack of dogs, however, and the pack usually loses its track, also because the scent of a fleeing hare reduces in intensity. Beagling is thus a sport where the prey has an honest chance of escaping. A pack of Beagles will also be used to track down foxes. This is "work." The Beagles take care that the fox flees to its own hole, or "in an emergency" into a rabbit burrow. The huntsmen then finish the job by using a terrier to drive the fox out of the hole

and catch it or kill it. Beagles are also excellent "bloodhounds" and can be used to track down wounded animals. A well-trained Beagle can pick up and follow the scent of a wounded animal, even after 48 hours, and this has become a sport which is practiced in Beagle trials.

Breed standard

A standard has been developed for all breeds recognized by the AKC (American Kennel Club). This standard provides a guideline for breeders and inspectors. It is something of an ideal that dogs of the breed must strive to match. With some breeds, dogs are already bred that match the ideal. Other breeds have a long way to go. There is a list of defects for each breed. These can be serious defects that disqualify the dog, and it will be excluded from breeding. Permitted defects are not serious, but do cost points in a show.

The American Kennel Club Breed Standard
Head
The skull should be fairly long, slightly domed at occiput, with cranium broad and full. *Ears:* Ears set on moderately low, long, reaching when drawn out nearly, if not quite, to the end of the nose; fine in texture, fairly broad-with almost entire absence of erectile power-setting close to the head,

with the forward edge slightly inturning to the cheek-rounded at tip. *Eyes:* Eyes large, set well apart-soft and houndlike-expression gentle and pleading; of a brown or hazel color. ***Muzzle:*** Muzzle of medium length-straight and square-cut—the stop moderately defined. *Jaws:* Level. Lips free from flews; nostrils large and open. *Defects:* A very flat skull, narrow across the top; excess of dome, eyes small, sharp and terrierlike, or prominent and protruding; muzzle long, snipy or cut away decidedly below the eyes, or very short. Roman-nosed, or upturned, giving a dish-face expression. Ears short, set on high or with a tendency to rise above the point of origin.

Body

Neck and Throat: Neck rising free and light from the shoulders strong in substance yet not loaded, of medium length. The throat clean and free from folds of skin; a slight wrinkle below the angle of the jaw, however, may be allowable. *Defects:* A thick, short, cloddy neck carried on a line with the top of the shoulders. Throat showing dewlap and folds of skin to a degree termed "throatiness."

Shoulders and Chest

Shoulders sloping-clean, muscular, not heavy or loaded-conveying the idea of freedom of action with activity and strength. Chest deep and broad, but not broad enough to interfere with the free play of the shoulders. *Defects:* Straight, upright shoulders. Chest disproportionately wide or with lack of depth.

Back, Loin and Ribs

Back short, muscular and strong. Loin broad and slightly arched, and the ribs well sprung, giving abundance of lung room. *Defects:* Very long or swayed or roached back. Flat, narrow loin. Flat ribs.

Forelegs and Feet

Forelegs: Straight, with plenty of bone in proportion to size of the hound. Pasterns short and straight. *Feet:* Close, round and firm. Pad full and hard. *Defect:* Out at elbows. Knees knuckled over forward, or bent backward. Forelegs crooked or Dachshundlike. Feet long, open or spreading.

Hips, Thighs, Hind Legs and Feet

Hips and thighs strong and well muscled, giving abundance of propelling power. Stifles strong and well let down. Hocks firm, symmetrical and moderately bent. Feet close and firm. *Defects:* Cowhocks, or straight hocks. Lack of muscle and propelling power. Open feet.

Tail

Set moderately high; carried gaily, but not turned forward

over the back; with slight curve; short as compared with size of the hound; with brush. **Defects:** A long tail. Teapot curve or inclined forward from the root. Rat tail with absence of brush.

Coat
A close, hard, hound coat of medium length. **Defects:** A short, thin coat, or of a soft quality.

Color
Any true hound color.

General Appearance
A miniature Foxhound, solid and big for his inches, with the wear-and-tear look of the hound that can last in the chase and follow his quarry to the death.

Scale of Points   (Total 100)
Head

Skull	5
Ears	10
Eyes	5
Muzzle	5
	25

Body

Neck	5
Chest and shoulders	15
Back, loin and ribs	15
	35

Running Gear

Forelegs	10
Hips, thighs and hind legs	10
Feet	10
	30

Coat	5
Stern	5

Varieties
There shall be two varieties: Thirteen Inch: which shall be for hounds not exceeding 13 inches in height. Fifteen Inch: which shall be for hounds over 13 but not exceeding 15 inches in height.

Disqualification
Any hound measuring more than 15 inches shall be disqualified.

Packs of Beagles
Score of points for judging:
Hounds

General levelness of pack	40%
Individual merit of hounds	30%
	70%
Manners	20%
Appointments	10%
Total	100%

Levelness of Pack
The first thing in a pack to be considered is that they present a unified appearance. The hounds must be as near to the same height, weight, conformation and color as possible.

Individual Merit of the Hounds
Is the individual bench-show quality of the hounds. A very level and sporty pack can be gotten together and not a single hound be a good Beagle. This is to be avoided.

Manners
The hounds must all work gaily

and cheerfully, with flags up-obeying all commands cheerfully. They should be broken to heel up, kennel up, follow promptly and stand. Cringing, sulking, lying down to be avoided. Also, a pack must not work as though in terror of master and whips. In Beagle packs it is recommended that the whip be used as little as possible.

Appointments
Master and whips should be dressed alike, the master or huntsman to carry horn—the whips and master to carry light thong whips. One whip should carry extra couplings on shoulder strap.

Recommendations for Show
Livery Black velvet cap, white stock, green coat, white breeches or knickerbockers, green or black stockings, white spats, black or dark brown shoes. Vest and gloves optional. Ladies should turn out exactly the same except for a white skirt instead of white breeches.
Approved September 10, 1957

Reproduced courtesy of the American Kennel Club.

Buying your Beagle

Once you've made that properly considered decision to buy a dog, there are several options. Should it be a puppy, an adult dog, or even an older dog?

Should it be a bitch or dog, a pedigree dog or a mixed breed? Of course, the question also comes up as to where to buy your dog-from a private person, a reliable breeder or an animal shelter? For you and the animal, it's vital to get these questions sorted out in advance. You want a dog that will fit your circumstances properly. Check with the breed association whether the Beagle is a suitable housemate for you. Or rather . . . does the Beagle want you?

With a puppy, you get a playful energetic housemate that will easily adapt to a new environment. If you want something quieter, an older dog is a good choice. The breed association offers a placing service, which you could use to offer a good new home for a Beagle that, for no fault of it's own, is looking for another master.

Pros and cons of the Beagle

The Beagle is a splendid, proud dog with bags of character. It is a strong and compact hound without giving a coarse impression. Its coloring, its happy nature, its soft and appealing face and that winning look in its eyes have captured countless many hearts. These dogs are loyal, good with children and other dogs. The Beagle is and will remain a hunting dog. They go crazy at the sight of a rabbit or hare and, if they pick up the scent of a rabbit, hare, or deer, their behavior changes immediately. Out in the fields, too, they show all the characteristics of a full-blooded hunter and will chase all kinds of prey. You must always have your dog well under control, otherwise you might wait for hours while your Beagle is away chasing rabbits and hares. Your presence is forgotten and it follows its nose barking incessantly. You need to understand that completely before buying a Beagle. These ancient characteristics, its passion for hunting and its independence (pigheadedness say many) and disobedience still cause many misunderstandings between dog and master.

At home, they are very affectionate, sometimes somewhat shy dogs. Beagles are friendly and soft by nature. They cling to their "pack," this being the family where the Beagle has "moved in." Beagles must be kept in the house and not in a kennel, otherwise they don't have the opportunity to build a good bond with the family-their pack!

As pack dogs they have a strong need for company and attention. A Beagle that is left alone too long will make its displeasure known, often in a very loud manner. It is therefore not a dog for a family where it will often be left alone for longer than two or three hours.

Of course, there are individual "nuances" in character within the breed, but never assume that your dog may benefit from these. Avoid disappointments for your dog and your family. In general the Beagle is a quiet, affectionate housemate, as long as it can satisfy its strong need for exercise. If you're not able to let your Beagle walk and run off the leash for one and a half to two hours a day, then certainly don't buy a Beagle.

Taking its strong self-willed nature into account, the Beagle needs training and a firm upbringing, but it is primarily its master that needs bringing up. A strong bond between master and dog must develop.

The Beagle as a house-pet

Its well-balanced nature and happy looks make the Beagle a good house-pet. Its size is manageable. Its short coat is maintenance free. It will leave hairs in the house, but a good brush is enough to keep its coat clean. Its character is soft. It likes to be heard, but is definitely not a watchdog. If it could, it would make any burglar a cup of coffee. It is small in size, but big in character and that needs to be kept in mind. As you have already read, the Beagle is an

independent hunting dog and thus needs a firm upbringing, which will certainly not always be easy. The saying "THINK BEFORE YOU ACT!" applies here, too. It is normally a soft-hearted, cheerful and mischievous rascal. At home, it shows itself as a wonderful smoocher, affectionate with everyone; outdoors, it becomes a hunter and is in its element if it can enthusiastically track a scent when out walking.

Because it has been bred for centuries as a dog to drive game to the huntsman without human help, the Beagle has a good portion of self-will, which some regard as pig-headedness.

All these character traits make a Beagle a dog that is difficult to raising and it needs a rigorous upbringing. We recommend that you follow an obedience course with your Beagle so that you can learn how to handle it. The Beagle also needs a lot of attention and expects this of its master and mistress. It's also not a dog that can easily be left alone, if at all. After all, the family is its pack and it feels comfortable with them. If the pack leaves the house, it's perfectly possible that the Beagle will turn the place upside down and it's understandable that a Beagle that is left alone for hours every day will pine away in its loneliness.

When considering buying a dog, you must also think about the costs that keeping a dog will involve. To give you some idea about what your Beagle companion might cost, we've put a number of items together for you.

Buying the puppy
Veterinarian's costs: several puppy examination and vaccination sessions and then annual examinations and vaccinations, regular worming, heartworm and flea/tick prevention, spaying or castration.
Food, drinking bowls, basket and leash. Insurance, if desired Dog license Kennel costs during your vacation if you can't take your companion with you.

With its happy nature, the Beagle is always in for a game. A box with knotted rope, a leg from an old pair of jeans, cloths, tennis balls and toilet rolls are often its favorite toys. Because it's a hunting dog, the Beagle needs a lot of exercise and must be allowed to run for at least an hour each day.

So if you as its master and mistress lead a busy life, then don't buy a Beagle. You will not have the time necessary to bring up your dog and give it the attention it needs and deserves.

Male or female?

Whether you choose a male or a female puppy, or an adult dog or bitch, is an entirely personal decision. A male typically needs more leadership because he tends to be more dominant in nature. He will try to play boss over other dogs and, if he gets the chance, over people too. In the wild, the most dominant dog (or wolf) is always the leader of the pack. In many cases this is a male. A bitch is much more focused on her master, she sees him as the pack leader.

A puppy test is good for defining what kind of character a young dog will develop. During a test one usually sees that a dog is more dominant than a bitch. You can often quickly recognize the bossy, the adventurous and the cautious characters. So visit the litter a couple of times early on. Try to pick a puppy that suits your own personality. A dominant dog, for instance, needs a strong hand. It will continuously try to see just how far it can go. You must regularly make it clear who's the boss, and that it must obey all the members of the family.

When bitches are sexually mature, they will go into season. On average, a bitch is in season twice a year for about two or three weeks. A bitch may be in a depressed mood during this period and may be less loyal and affectionate. This is the fertile period when she can be mated. Particularly in the second half of her season, she will want to go looking for a dog to mate with, and she can also become pregnant. The male, on the other hand, is better balanced and does not suffer hormone swings.

A male dog will show more masculine traits once he is sexually mature. He will make sure other dogs know what territory is his by urinating as often as possible in as many places as he can. He is also difficult to restrain if there's a bitch in season nearby. As far as normal care is concerned, there is little difference between a dog and a bitch.

With the Beagle the decision for male or female is wide open. Both are affectionate, loyal and mischievous. There is little difference as far as upbringing is concerned. The male may display some "macho" traits, but don't underestimate the ladies either.

Puppy or adult?
After you've made the decision for a male or female, the next question comes up. Should it be a puppy or an adult dog? Your family circumstances usually play a major role here.

Of course, it's great having a

sweet little puppy in the house, but bringing up a young dog costs a lot of time. In the first year of its life it learns more than during the rest of its life. This is the period when the foundations are laid for elementary matters such as house-training, obedience and social behavior. You must reckon with the fact that your puppy will keep you busy for a couple of hours a day, certainly in the first few months. You won't need so much time with a grown dog. It has already been brought up (but this doesn't mean it won't need correcting from time to time!).

A puppy will no doubt leave a trail of destruction in its wake for the first few months. With a little bad luck, this will cost you a number of rolls of wallpaper, some good shoes and a few socks. In the worst case you'll be left with some chewed furniture. Some puppies even manage to tear drapes from their rails. With good upbringing this "vandalism" will quickly disappear, but you might not have to worry about this if you get an older dog.

The greatest advantage of a puppy, of course, is that you can bring it up your own way. And the upbringing a dog gets (or doesn't get) is a major influence on its whole character. Finally, financial aspects may play a role in your choice. A puppy is generally (much) more expensive than an adult dog, not only in purchase price but also in "maintenance." A puppy needs to go to the veterinarian more often for the necessary vaccinations and check-ups.

Overall, bringing up a puppy costs a good deal of energy, time and money, but you have its upbringing in your own hands. An adult dog costs less money and time, but its character is already formed. You should also try to find out about the background of an adult dog. Its previous owner may have formed its character in somewhat less positive ways.

Two dogs?

Having two or more dogs in the house is not just nice for us, but also for the animals themselves. Dogs get a lot of pleasure from their own company. After all, they are pack animals. If you're sure that you want two young dogs, it's best not to buy them at the same time. Bringing a dog up and establishing the bond between dog and master takes time, and you need to give a lot of attention to your dog in this phase. Having two puppies in the house means you have to divide your attention between them. Apart from that, there's a danger that they will focus on one another rather than on their master. Buy the second pup when the first is (almost) an adult.

Two adult dogs can happily be brought into the home together. Getting a puppy when the first dog is somewhat older often has a positive effect on the older dog. The influence of the puppy almost seems to give it a second childhood. The older dog, if it's been well brought up, can help with the up-bringing of the puppy. Young dogs like to imitate the behavior of their elders. Don't forget to give both dogs the same amount of attention. Take the puppy out alone at least once per day during the first eighteen months. Give the older dog enough opportunity to get some peace and quiet. It won't want an enthusiastic youngster running around under its feet all the time.

The combination of a male and female needs special attention. If you don't want puppies from your dogs (i.e. never, definitely), you must take measures to stop this happening. Besides "spaying" (sterilizing) the female, castrating the male is also an option.

A dog and children

Beagles and children are a great combination. They can play together and get great pleasure out of each other's company. Moreover, children need to learn how to handle living beings; they develop respect and a sense of responsibility by caring for a dog (or other pets). However sweet a dog is, children must understand that it is an animal and not a toy. A dog isn't comfortable when it's messed around with. It can become frightened, timid and even aggressive. So make it clear what a dog likes and what it doesn't, such as having its ears or tail pulled or being disturbed when it's eating. Look for ways the child can play with the dog, perhaps a game of hide and seek where the child hides and the dog has to find it. Even a simple tennis ball can give enormous pleasure. Children must learn to leave a dog in peace when it doesn't want to play any more. The dog must also have its own place where it's not disturbed. Have children help with your dog's care as much as possible. A strong bond will be the result.

The arrival of a baby also means changes in the life of a dog. Before the birth you can help get the dog acquainted with the new situation. Let it sniff at the new things in the house and it will quickly accept them. When the baby has arrived, involve the dog as much as possible in day-by-day events, but make sure it gets plenty of attention too. NEVER leave a dog alone with young children. Crawling infants sometimes make unexpected movements, which can easily frighten a dog. And infants are hugely curious, and may try to find out whether the tail is really fastened to the dog, or whether its eyes come out, just like they do with their cuddly toys. But a dog is a dog and it will defend itself when it feels threatened. A dog can't talk after all and only has its teeth to make a point with.

Where to buy

There are various ways to acquire a dog. The decision for a puppy or an adult dog will also define for the most part where to buy your dog. If it's to be a puppy, then you need to find a breeder with a litter. If you chose a popular breed, like the Beagle, there is choice enough. But you may also face the problem that there are so many puppies on sale that have only been bred for profit's sake. You can see how many puppies are for sale by looking in the newspaper. Some of these dogs have a pedigree, but many don't. Breeders often don't watch out for breed-specific illnesses and in-breeding; puppies are separated from their mother as fast as possible and are thus insufficiently socialized. Never buy a puppy that is too young, or whose mother you weren't able to see.

Fortunately, there are also enough bona-fide breeders of Beagles. Try to visit a number of breeders before you actually buy your puppy. Ask if the breeder is prepared to help you after you've bought your puppy, and to help you find solutions for any problems that may come up. The breed association will put breeders and aspiring owners in contact with each other. People looking for a Beagle can be put on a waiting list. As soon as there is a breeder with puppies available, the potential buyer is notified. Beagles are sought after dogs and you may need to wait before you get your puppy.

Finally, you should be aware that pedigree certificates are also issued for the offspring of animals with hereditary defects, or those that have not been examined for these. A pedigree says nothing about the health of the animals bred.

If you're looking for an adult dog, it's best to contact the breed association, who often help place adult dogs that can no longer be kept by their owners because of personal circumstances (impulse buying, moving home, divorce etc.).

Things to watch out for

Buying a puppy is no simple matter. You must pay attention to the following:
• Never buy a puppy on impulse, even if it is love at first sight. A dog is a living being that will need care and attention over a long period. It is not a toy that you can put away when you're done with it.
• Take a good look at the mother. Is she calm, nervous, aggressive, well cared-for or neglected? The behavior and condition of the mother is not only a sign of the quality of the breeder, but also of the puppy you're about to buy.
• Avoid buying a puppy whose mother has been kept only in a kennel. A young dog needs as many different impressions as possible in its first few months, including living in a family group. It gets used to people and possibly other pets. Kennel dogs miss these experiences and are inadequately socialized.
• Always ask to see the parents' papers (vaccination certificates, pedigrees, official reports on health examinations).
• Never buy a puppy younger than eight weeks.
• Always put all agreements with the breeder in writing, the breed association has a model agreement for this purpose.
• Ask your breeder about any hereditary diseases such as epilepsy, disk disease or heart abnormalities that the parent dogs may have suffered from.
• We recommend buying a puppy with guidance from the breed association.

Traveling with your Beagle

There are a few things to think about before traveling with your dog. While one dog may enjoy traveling, another may hate it. You may like vacations in far-away places, but it's questionable is whether your dog will agree with you.

That very first trip

The first trip of a puppy's life is also the most nerve-wracking. This is the trip from the breeder's to its new home. Try to pick your puppy up early in the morning. It then has plenty of time to get used to its new situation. Ask the breeder not to feed it that day. The young animal will be overwhelmed by all kinds of new experiences. Firstly, it's away from its mother; it's in a small room (the car) with all its different smells, noises and strange people.

So there's a big chance that the puppy will be car-sick this first time, with the annoying consequence that it will remember riding in the car as an unpleasant experience.

So it's important to make this first trip as pleasant as possible. When picking up a puppy, always take someone with you who can sit in the back seat with the puppy on his or her lap and talk to it calmly. If it's too warm for the puppy, a place on the floor at the feet of your companion is ideal. The pup will lie there relatively quietly and may even take a nap. Ask the breeder for a cloth or something else from its nest that carries a familiar scent. The puppy can lie on this in the car, and it will also help if it feels alone during the first nights at home.

If the trip home is a long one, then stop for a break (once in a while). Let your puppy roam and sniff around (on the leash!), have a little drink and, if necessary, do its business. Do take care to lay an old towel in the car. It can happen that the puppy, in its nervousness, may urinate or be sick. It's also good advice to give a puppy positive experiences with car journeys. Make short trips to nice places where you can walk and play with it. A dog that doesn't like riding in a car can cause a lot of problems.

Taking your Beagle on vacation

When making vacation plans, you also need to think about what you're going to do with your dog during that time. Are you taking it with you, putting it into a kennel or leaving it with friends? In any event there are a number of things you need to do in good time.

If you want to take your dog with you, you need to be sure in good time that it will be welcome at your vacation home, and what the rules there are. If you're going overseas, it will need certain vaccinations and a health certificate, which normally need to be done at least four weeks before departure. Your veterinarian can give you the most recent information.

If your trip is to a tick infested area, ask for a treatment against ticks (you can read more about this in the *Parasites* chapter).

Although dog-owners usually enjoy taking their dog on vacation, you must seriously ask yourself whether the dog feels that way, too. Dogs certainly don't always feel comfortable in a hot country. Days spent riding in a car are also often not their preference, and some dogs suffer badly from car-sickness. There are good medications for this, but it's questionable whether you're doing your dog a favor with them. If you do decide to take it with you, make regular stops at safe places during your trip, so that your dog can have a good run. Take plenty of fresh drinking water with you, as well as the food your dog is used to. Don't leave your dog in the car standing in the sun. It can quickly be overcome by the heat, with even fatal consequences. If you can't avoid it, park the car in the shade if at all possible, and leave a window open for a little fresh air. Even if you've taken these precautions, never stay away long, for dogs should really never be left in the car.

If you're traveling by plane or ship, make sure in good time that your dog can travel with you and what rules you need to observe. You will need some time to make all the arrangements. Maybe you decide not to take your dog with you, and you then need to find somewhere for it to stay. Arrangements for a place in kennels need to be made well in advance, and there may be certain vaccinations required, which need to be given a minimum of one month before the stay.

If your dog can't be accommodated in the homes of relatives or friends, it might be possible to have an acquaintance stay in your

house. This also needs to be arranged well in advance, as it may be difficult to find someone that can do this.

Always ensure that your dog can be traced should it run away or get lost while on vacation. A tag with home and

vacation address can prevent a lot of problems.

Moving

Dogs generally become more attached to humans than to the house they live in. Changing residence is usually not a problem for them. But, it can be useful before moving to let the dog get to know its new home and the area around it, if this is possible.

If you can, leave your dog with relatives or friends (or in a kennel) on the day of the move. The chance of it running away or getting lost is then practically non-existent. When your move is complete, you can pick your dog up and let it quietly get familiar with its new home and environment. Give it its own place in the house at once and it will quickly adapt. During the first week or so, always walk your dog on a leash because an animal can also get lost in new surroundings. Always take a different route so it quickly gets to know the neighborhood.

Don't forget to get your new address and phone number engraved on the dog's tag. Send a change of address notice to the institution that has any chip or tattoo data. Dogs must sometimes be registered in a new community, and you must pay for a dog license.

Nutrition, and feeding your Beagle

A dog will actually eat a lot more than just meat.

In the wild it would eat its prey complete with skin and fur, including the bones, stomach, and the innards with their semi-digested vegetable material. In this way the dog supplements its meat menu with the vitamins and minerals it needs. This is also the basis for feeding a domestic dog.

Ready-made foods

It's not easy for a layman to put together a complete menu for a dog, with all the necessary proteins, fats, vitamins and minerals in just the right proportions and quantities. Meat alone is certainly not a complete meal for a dog. It contains too little calcium. A calcium deficiency over time will lead to bone defects, and for a fast-growing puppy this can lead to serious skeleton deformities. If you put its food together yourself, you can easily give your dog too much in terms of vitamins and minerals, which can also be bad for your dog's health. You can avoid these problems by giving it ready-made food of a good brand. These products are well-balanced and contain everything your dog needs. Supplements such as vitamin preparations are superfluous. The amount of food your dog needs depends on its weight and activity level. You can find guidelines on the packaging.

Split the food into two meals per day if possible, and always make fresh water available for your pet. Because the food needs of a dog vary depending on its age and way of life, there is a complete range of dog food available. Your veterinarian can help you choose the appropriate food. There is a special puppy food made for medium breed puppies like the Beagle. There are high energy foods made for active dogs such as hunting dogs. Reduced calorie foods are available for less-active or overweight dogs, and a senior diet is available for older dogs. Again, consult your veterinarian for advice on the proper diet.

Always ensure there's a bowl of fresh drinking water available. Give your dog the time to digest its food and don't let it outside immediately after a meal. A dog should also never play on a full stomach. This can cause stomach torsion (stomach twisting), which can be fatal for your dog.

Canned and dry foods
Ready-made foods available at pet stores or in the supermarket can roughly be split into two

types: canned food and dry food. Whichever form you choose, ensure that it's a complete food with all the necessary substances. You can see this on the packaging.

Most dogs love canned food. Although the better brands are composed well, they do have one disadvantage: they are soft. A dog fed only on canned food will sooner or later have problems with its teeth (plaque, tartar, and periodontal disease). Besides canned food, give your dog hard foods at certain times or a dog chew. The advantage of dry foods is that they are hard, forcing the dog to use its jaws, removing plaque and massaging the gums, thus helping keep the teeth clean and strong. Dry foods are also easier to take with you when traveling. Always take a bottle of clean water with you on a trip.

Dog chew products
Naturally, once in a while you want to spoil your dog with something extra. Don't give it pieces of cheese or sausage as these contain too much salt and fat. There are various products available that a dog will find delicious and which are also healthy, especially for its teeth. You'll find a large range of varying quality in the pet store. The butcher's left-overs The bones of slaughtered

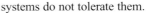

butcher's left-overs

animals have traditionally been given to the dog, and dogs are crazy about them, but they are not without risks. Pork and poultry bones are too weak. They can splinter and cause serious injury to the intestines. Beef bones are more suitable, but they must first be cooked to kill off dangerous bacteria. Pet stores carry a range of smoked and cooked beef and pork products such as pig ears and cow hooves. Feed these in moderation; some animals do not tolerate them well.

Fresh meat

If you do want to give your dog fresh meat occasionally, **never** give it raw, but always boiled or roasted. Raw (or not fully cooked) beef, pork, or chicken can contain life-threatening bacteria.

Rawhide chews

Dog chews are mostly made of beef or buffalo hide. Chews are usually knotted or pressed hide. A Beagle always needs plenty to chew on, especially as a puppy, in play or when its teeth are changing. Its gums then itch and its mouth is sensitive. It often feels uncomfortable during this period. Lots of distraction, exercise and attention for your dog will prevent corners chewed out of the sofa and carpets. These rawhide chews are also made in the shapes of shoes, twisted sticks, balls and various other shapes. Use rawhide chews in moderation; some dogs' digestive

systems do not tolerate them.

Munchy sticks

Munchy sticks are green, yellow, red or brown colored sticks of varying thickness. They consist of ground buffalo hide with a number of often-undefined additives. The composition and quality of these between-meal treats is not always clear. Some are fine, but there have also been sticks found to contain high levels of cardboard and even paint residues. Choose a product whose ingredients are clearly described.

Overweight?

Recent investigations have shown that many dogs are overweight. A dog usually gets fat because of over-feeding and lack of exercise. Use of medications or a disease is

Munchy sticks

rarely the cause. Dogs that get too fat are often given too much food or treats between meals. Gluttony or boredom can also be a cause, and a dog often puts on weight following castration or spaying. Due to changes in hormone levels, it becomes less active and consumes less energy. Finally, simply too little exercise alone can lead to a dog becoming overweight. You will be surprised how happy your dog will be when it gets back to its "normal" weight.

You can use the following rule of thumb to check whether your dog is overweight: you should be able to feel its ribs, but not see them. If you can't feel its ribs then your dog is overweight. Overweight dogs live a passive life, they play too little and tire quickly. They

can also suffer from all kinds of medical problems such as orthopedic problems, disk disease, heart disease, diabetes, and a shortened life span.

So it's important to make sure your dog doesn't get overweight. Always follow the guidelines on food packaging. Adapt them if your dog is less active or gets lots of snacks. Try to make sure your dog gets plenty of exercise by playing and running with it as much as you can. If your dog starts to show signs of putting on weight you can switch to a low-calorie food. If it's really overweight and reducing its food quantity doesn't help, then a special diet is the only solution Your veterinarian can recommend the diet appropriate for weight loss.

Rawhide chews

Caring for your Beagle

Good (daily) care is extremely important for your dog. A well-cared for dog is less likely to get sick.

Caring for your dog is not only necessary but also a pleasure. Master and dog are giving each other some attention, and it's an excellent opportunity for a game and a hug.

The coat
Caring for your dog's coat involves regular brushing and combing, together with checking for parasites such as fleas and ticks. How often a dog needs to be brushed and combed depends on the length of its coat. Use the right equipment for taking care of the coat. Combs should not be too sharp and you should use a rubber or natural hairbrush. Always comb from the head back towards the tail, following the direction of the hair.

If you get a puppy used to being brushed from an early age, it will enjoy having its coat cared for. Only bathe a dog when it's really necessary, usually once every four weeks to avoid stripping the coat of its natural protective oils. Always use a special dog shampoo and make sure it doesn't get into the dog's eyes or ears. Rinse the suds out thoroughly. Only let your dog outdoors again when it's completely dry.

A veterinarian can prescribe special medicinal shampoos for some skin conditions. Always follow the instructions to the letter.

Good flea prevention is highly important to avoid skin and coat problems. Fleas must be treated not only on the dog itself but also in its surroundings (see the chapter Parasites). Coat problems can also occur due to an allergy to certain food substances. In such cases, a veterinarian can prescribe a hypoallergenic diet.

Teeth

A dog must be able to eat properly to stay in good condition, so it needs healthy teeth. Check its teeth regularly. Get in touch with your veterinarian if you suspect that all is not well. A regular diet of hard dry food can help keep your dog's teeth clean and healthy. There are special dog chews on the market that help prevent plaque and help keep the animal's breath fresh.

Best of all is regular tooth brushing. You can use special toothbrushes for dogs, but a finger wrapped in a small piece of gauze will also do the job. Get your dog used to having its teeth cleaned at an early age and you won't have problems. Never use human toothpaste. Your veterinarian or pet store can provide you with toothpaste formulated especially for dogs.

You can even teach an older dog to have its teeth cleaned. With a dog chew as a reward it will certainly be happy.

Nails

On a dog that regularly walks on hard surfaces, its nails usually grind themselves down. In this case there's no need to clip their nails. But it wouldn't

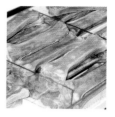

Chewing is also good for cleaning teeth

do any harm to check their length now and again, especially on dogs that don't get out on the streets often. Using a piece of paper, you can easily see whether its nails are too long. If you can push the paper between the nail and the ground when the dog is standing, then the nail is the right length.

Nails that are too long can bother a dog. It can injure itself when scratching, so they must be kept trimmed. You can buy special nail clippers in pet stores. Be careful not to clip back too far as you could damage the cuticle, which can bleed profusely. If you feel unsure, have this necessary task done by a veterinarian or pet groomer.

Special attention is needed for the extra nail on the side of the rear paws, the so-called dewclaw. This nail does not touch the ground and thus does not wear itself down. You must clip this nail back regularly or your dog may get caught on it. Note that some dogs to not have dewclaws.

Eyes

A dog's eyes should be cleaned daily. Mucus discharge and little lumps of dried eye moisture can get into the corners of the eye. You can easily remove them by wiping them downward with your thumb. If you don't like doing that, use a piece of tissue or toilet paper.

Keeping your dog's eyes clean will take only a few seconds a day, so do it every day. If the discharge becomes yellow and slimy, this points to heavy irritation or an infection. Seek veterinary care for this condition.

Ears

The ears are often forgotten when caring for dogs, but they must be checked at least once a week. Beagles are especially prone to ear infections since their floppy ears cover the opening of the ear canal. If its ears are very dirty or have too much wax, you must clean them. This should preferably be done with a clean cotton cloth, moistened with lukewarm water or baby oil. NEVER penetrate the ear canal with an object. If hair in the ears causes problems, it's best to remove it. Carefully pull it out using your thumb and index finger. If you do neglect cleaning your dog's ears there's a substantial risk of infection. A dog that is constantly scratching at its ears might be suffering from dirty ears, an ear infection or ear mites, making a visit to the veterinarian essential.

Raising your Beagle

The Beagle is a dog with real character. If you can handle it and give it what it deserves, then you have a loyal companion for life.

It is very important that your Beagle is properly raised and is obedient. Not only will this bring you more pleasure, but it's also nicer for your environment. A puppy can learn what it may and may not do by playing. Rewards and consistency are important tools in bringing up a dog. Reward it with your voice, a stroke or something tasty and it will quickly learn to obey. A puppy-training course can also help you along the way.

A strong bond must develop between master and dog. This can be created by spending a lot of time together, without making the dog mistrustful with too harsh a hand. This helps the combination of man and dog whenever you want to take part in hunt training, obedience courses and/or agility competitions.

The master must be a real leader, otherwise the Beagle will be happy to take control itself. Its master must be consistent in insisting that his command be followed and he needs plenty of patience. Authority is everything and this requires a good deal of self-discipline and effort.

Disobedience (and running away) must be countered by constant attention to the dog and its environment. Then you can intervene just at the right time. You can only enforce a command if the dog is close at hand, otherwise it's best not to call a command at all. If your dog does run away, wait until it returns without calling or whistling, and then reward it.

Because the Beagle has been bred for centuries as a dog that can bring game to the huntsman without human help, it possesses a large portion of independence, that we may regard as a portion of pig-headedness.

These character traits make the Beagle a dog that is difficult to bring up, and we recommend an obedience course with the Beagle, so that its master can learn how to handle his dog properly. Whether the Beagle will apply what it has learned in practice is another question. It remains an affectionate, mischievous hunting dog that will first do what it wants, such as tracking down the scent of a cat or rabbit. Your dog should be quite obedient before it has reached the age of seven months, because then its hunting instinct starts to develop and its passion for the hunt appears. You, as its master, must take this characteristic as the starting point for a good upbringing. If you can't or don't want to do this, you must NEVER buy a Beagle.

Exercise

Your Beagle needs PLENTY of exercise. But don't overdo things when it's a puppy or very young dog. Once it's full grown, daily walks of 1.5 to 2 hours are no luxury. If it doesn't get that much exercise then it's a foregone conclusion that your Beagle will spend its excess energy on your expensive furniture. If you don't have a lot of time for your dog, if you work a lot and your dog must be alone longer than two to three hours a day, then don't get a Beagle.

(Dis)obedience

A dog that won't obey you is not just a problem for you, but also for your surroundings. It's therefore important to avoid unwanted behavior. In fact, this is what training your dog is all about, so get started early. "Start 'em young!" applies to dogs too. An untrained dog is not just a nuisance, but can also cause dangerous situations, running into the road, chasing joggers or jumping at people. A dog must be trained out of this undesirable behavior as quickly as possible. The longer you let it go on, the more difficult it will become to correct. The best thing to do is to attend a special obedience course. Not only will this help to correct the dog's behavior, but its owner also learns how to handle undesirable behavior at home. A dog must not only obey its master during training, but at home, too.

Always be consistent when training good behavior and correcting annoying behavior. This means a dog may always behave in a certain way, or must never behave that way. Reward it for good behavior and never punish it after the fact for any wrongdoing. If your dog finally comes to you after you've been calling it a long time, then reward it. If you're angry because you had to wait so long, it may feel it's actually being punished for coming. It will probably not obey at all the next time for fear of punishment.

Try to take no notice of undesirable behavior. Your dog will perceive your reaction (even a negative one) as a reward for this behavior. If you need to correct the dog, then do this immediately. Use your voice or grip it by the scruff of its neck and push it to the ground. This is the way a mother dog calls her pups to order. What also helps with a Beagle is to grab it by the scruff of its neck immediately after the wrongdoing and put it outside. It has now been ejected by its pack and will not like that. A condition is that your yard is Beagle-proof, because once outside, a Beagle will immediately become a hunter that will go off hunting alone.

Rewards for good behavior are, by far, preferable to punishment;

they always get a better result.

House-training

The very first training (and one of the most important) that a dog needs is house-training. The basis for good house-training is keeping a good eye on your puppy. If you pay attention, you will notice that it will sniff a long time and do turns around a certain spot before doing its business there. Pick it up gently and place it outside, always at the same place. Reward it abundantly if it does its business there.

Another good moment for house-training is after eating or sleeping. A puppy often needs to do its business at these times. Let it relieve itself before playing with it, otherwise it will forget to do so and you'll not reach your goal. For the first few days, take your puppy out for a walk just after it's eaten or woken up. It will quickly learn the meaning, especially if it's rewarded with a dog cookie for a successful attempt. Of course, it's not always possible to go out after every snack or snooze. Lay newspapers at different spots in the house. Whenever the pup needs to do its business, place it on a newspaper. After some time it will start to look for a place itself. Then start to reduce the number of newspapers until there is just one left, at the front or back door. The puppy will learn to go to the door if it needs to relieve itself. Then you put it on the leash and go out with it. Finally you can remove the last newspaper. Your puppy is now house-trained.

One thing that certainly won't work is punishing an accident after the fact. A dog whose nose is rubbed in its urine or its droppings won't understand that at all. It will only get frightened of you. Rewarding works much better than punishment. An indoor kennel or crate can be a good tool to help in house-training. A puppy won't foul its own nest, so a crate can be a good solution for the night, or during periods in the day when you can't watch it. But a crate must not become a jail where your dog is locked up day and night.

First exercises

The basic commands for an obedient dog are those for sit, lie down, come and stay. But a puppy should first learn its name. Use it as much as possible from the first day on followed by a friendly "Come!" Reward it with your voice and a stroke when it comes to you. Your puppy will quickly recognize the intention and has now learned its first command in a playful manner. Don't be too harsh with a young puppy, and don't always punish it immediately if it doesn't always react in the right way. When you

call your puppy to you in this way have it come right to you. You can teach a pup to sit by holding a piece of dog cookie above his nose and then slowly moving it backwards. The puppy's head will also move backwards until its hind legs slowly go down. At that moment you call "Sit!" After a few attempts, it will quickly know this nice game. Use the Sit! command before you give your dog its food, put it on the leash, or before it's allowed to cross the street.

Teaching the command to lie down is similar. Instead of moving the piece of dog cookie backwards, move it down vertically until your hand reaches the ground and then forwards. The dog will also move its forepaws forwards and lie down on its own. At that moment call "Lie down!" or "Lay!" This command is useful when you want a dog to be quiet.

Two people are needed for the Come! command. One holds the dog back while the other runs away. After about forty feet or so, he stops and enthusiastically calls "Come!" The other person now lets the dog free, and it should obey the command at once. Again you reward it abundantly. The Come! command is useful in many situations and good for safety too.

A dog learns to stay from the

sitting or lying position. While its sitting or lying down, you call the command: "Stay!" and then step back one step. If the dog moves with you, quietly put it back in position, without displaying anger. If you do react angrily, you're actually punishing it for coming to you, and you'll only confuse your dog. It can't understand that coming is rewarded one time, and punished another. Once the dog stays nicely reward it abundantly. Practice this exercise with increasing distances (at first no more than three feet). The Stay! command is useful when getting out of the car.

Courses

Obedience courses to help you bring up your dog are available across the country. These courses are not just informative, but also fun for dog and master.

With a puppy, you can begin with a puppy course. This is designed to provide the basic training. A puppy that has attended such a course has learned about all kinds of things that will confront it in later life: other dogs, humans, traffic and what these mean. The puppy will also learn obedience and to follow a number of basic commands. Apart from all that, attention will be given to important subjects such as brushing, being alone, riding in a car, and doing its

business in the right places. The next step after a puppy course is a course for young dogs. This course repeats the basic exercises and ensures that the growing dog doesn't get into bad habits. After this, the dog can move on to an obedience course for full-grown dogs. For more information on where to find courses in your area, contact your local kennel club.

Play and toys

There are various ways to play with your dog, You can romp and run with it, but also play a number of games, such as retrieving, tug-of-war, hide-and-seek and catch. A tennis ball is ideal for retrieving, you can play tug-of-war with an old sock or a special tugging rope. Start with tug-of-war only after your dog is a year old. A puppy must first get its second teeth and then they need several months to strengthen. There's a real chance of your dog's teeth becoming deformed if you start too young. You can use almost anything for a game of hide-and-seek. A frisbee is ideal for catching games. Never use too small a ball for games. It can easily get lodged in the dog's throat.

Its cheerful character means a Beagle is always ready for a game. Favorite toys are an old sock with a tennis ball inside, a leg of an old pair of jeans with a knot in it, toilet rolls, tennis balls and cotton rags. They cost nothing and your Beagle will love them.

Play is extremely important. Not only does it strengthen the bond between dog and master, but it's also healthy for both. Make sure that you're the one that ends the game. Only stop when the dog has brought back the ball or frisbee, and make sure you always win the tug-of-war. This confirms your dominant position in the hierarchy. Use these toys only during play so that the dog doesn't forget their significance. When choosing a special dog toy, remember that dogs are hardly careful with them. So always buy toys of good quality that a dog can't easily destroy.

Be very careful with sticks and twigs. The latter, particularly, can easily splinter. A splinter of wood in your dog's throat or intestines can cause awful problems. Throwing sticks or twigs can also be dangerous. If they stick into the ground a dog can easily run into them with an open mouth.

If you would like to do more than just play games, you can now also play sports with your dog. For people who want to do more, there are various other sporting alternatives such as flyball, agility, and obedience.

Aggressiveness

Beagles are practically never aggressive. But even they can sometimes be difficult with other animals or people, so it's good to understand more about the

background of aggression in dogs.

There are two different types of canine aggressive behavior: anxious-aggressive and dominant-aggressive. An anxious-aggressive dog can be recognized by its pulled back ears and its low position. It will have pulled in its lips, showing its teeth. This dog is aggressive because it's very frightened and feels cornered. It would prefer to run away, but if it can't then it will bite to defend itself. It will grab its victim anywhere it can. The attack is usually brief and, as soon as the dog can see a way to escape, it's gone. In a confrontation with other dogs, it will normally turn out as the loser. It can become even more aggressive once it's realized that people or other dogs are afraid of it. This behavior cannot be easily corrected . First you have to try and understand what the dog is afraid of. Professional advice is a good idea here because the wrong approach can easily make the problem worse.

The dominant-aggressive dog's body language is different. Its ears stand up and its tail is raised and stiff. This dog will always go for its victim's arms, legs or throat. It is extremely self-assured and highly-placed in the dog hierarchy. Its attack is a display of power rather than a consequence of fear. This dog needs to know who's boss. You must bring it up rigorously and with a strong hand. An obedience course can help.

A dog may also bite itself because it's in pain. This is a natural defensive reaction. In this case try to resolve the dog's fear as far as possible. Reward him for letting you get to the painful spot. Be careful, because a dog in pain may also bite its master! Muzzling it can help prevent problems if you have to do something that may be painful. Never punish a dog for this type of aggression!

Fear

The source of anxious behavior can often be traced to the first weeks of a dog's life. A shortage of new experiences during this important phase (also called the "socialization phase") has great influence on its later behavior. A dog that never encountered humans, other dogs or animals during the socialization phase will be afraid of them later. This fear is common in dogs brought up in a barn or kennel, with almost no contact with humans. As we saw, fear can lead to aggressive behavior, so it's important that a puppy gets as many new impressions as possible in the first weeks of its life. Take it with you into town in the car or on the bus, walk it down busy streets and allow it to have plenty of contact with people, other dogs and other animals. It's a huge task to turn an anxious, poorly socialized dog into a real pet. It will probably take an enormous amount of attention, love, patience and energy to get such an animal used to everything around it. Reward it often and give it plenty of time to adapt and, over time, it will learn to trust you and become less anxious. Try not to force anything, because that will always have the reverse effect. Here, too, an obedience course can help a lot. A dog can be especially afraid of strangers. Have visitors give it something tasty as a treat. Put a can of dog cookies by the door so that your visitors can spoil your dog when they arrive. Again, don't try to force anything. If the dog is still frightened, leave it in peace.

Dogs are often frightened in certain situations; well-known examples are thunderstorms and fireworks. In these cases ignore their anxious behavior. If you react to their whimpering and whining, it's the same as rewarding it. If you ignore its fear completely, the dog will quickly learn that nothing is wrong. You can speed up this "learning process" by rewarding its positive behavior.

Rewarding

Rewarding forms the basis for bringing up a dog. Rewarding good behavior works far better than punishing bad behavior and rewarding is also much more fun. Over time, the opinions on upbringing for dogs have gradually changed. In the past the proper way to correct bad behavior was regarded as a sharp pull on the leash. Today, experts view rewards as a positive incentive to get dogs to do what we expect of them. There are many ways to reward a dog. The usual ways are a stroke or a friendly word, even without a tasty treat to go with it. Of course, a piece of dog cookie does wonders when you're training a puppy. Be sure you always have something delicious in your pocket to reward good behavior. Another form of reward is play. Whenever a dog notices you have a ball in your pocket, it won't go far from your side. As soon as you've finished playing, put the ball away. This way your dog will always do its best in exchange for a game.

Despite the emphasis you put on rewarding good behavior, a dog can sometimes be a nuisance or disobedient. You must correct such behavior immediately. Always be consistent: once "no" must always be "no."

Barking

Beagles are not watchdogs and generally are not dogs that bark too much or too often. Dogs that bark too much and too often are a nuisance for their surroundings. A dog-owner may tolerate barking up to a point, but neighbors are often annoyed by the unnecessary noise. Don't encourage your puppy to bark and yelp. Of course, it should be able to announce its presence, but if it goes on barking it must be called to order with a strict "Quiet!" If a puppy fails to obey, just hold its muzzle closed with your hand.

A dog will sometimes bark for long periods when left alone. It feels threatened and tries to get someone's attention by barking. There are special training programs for this problem, where dogs learn that being alone is nothing to be afraid of, and that its master will always return.

You can practice this with your dog at home. Leave the room and come back in at once. Reward your dog if it stays quiet. Gradually increase the length of your absences and keep rewarding it as long as it remains quiet. Never punish the dog if it does bark or yelp. It will never understand punishment afterwards, and this will only make the problem worse. Never go back into the room as long as your dog is barking, as it will view this as a reward. You might want to make the dog feel more comfortable by switching the

radio on for company during your absence. It will eventually learn that you always come back and the barking will reduce. If you don't get the required result, attend an obedience course.

Undesirable behavior

Beagles do not really display undesirable behavior by nature. But the Beagle does have a high-spirited and cheerful character. It will often greet people it knows, and those it doesn't, exuberantly and loudly, and can stand a robust game with its friends. Because the Beagle has been bred for centuries as a dog that can bring game to the huntsman without human help, it possesses a certain amount of independence, as well as a sure portion of pig-headedness, which many people find annoying when dealing with their Beagle. Owners who regard this as undesirable behavior certainly started out with this breed with the wrong expectations.

A Beagle is not a lapdog that will happily lay in its basket all day. It is, and will remain, a hunting dog that must be able to run free for a minimum of one hour per day, and hates being alone. Undesirable behavior is usually the result of insufficient exercise and/or attention, or the result of being alone too long and too often.

Reproduction

Dogs, and thus also the Beagle, follow their instincts, and reproduction is one of nature's important processes. For people who enjoy breeding dogs this is a positive circumstance.

Those who simply want a cozy companion however, will miss the regular adventures with females in heat and unrestrainable males like a toothache. But knowing a little about reproduction in dogs will help you to understand why they behave the way they do, and what measures you need to take when this happens.

Breeding recommendations

Breeding dogs is not just simply 1+1 = many. If you're planning to breed your Beagle, consult with your local kennel club for guidelines.

The kennel clubs place strict conditions on animals used for breeding. They must be examined for possible congenital defects. (See the chapter Your Beagle's health.) The breeder then must meet the requirements for reasonable care. If you breed a litter and sell the puppies without having carried out these checks, the new owners can hold you liable for any costs resulting from congenital defects, and these (veterinary) costs can be high! So contact the breeder of your female or the breed association if you plan to breed a litter of Beagles.

The female in season

Bitches become sexually mature at about eight to twelve months. Then they go into season for the first time. They are "in heat" for two to three weeks. During this period they discharge little drops of blood and they are very attractive to males. The bitch is fertile during the second half of her season, and will accept a male to mate. The best time for mating is then between the ninth and thirteenth day of her season. A female's first season is often shorter and less severe than those that follow. If you do want to breed your female you must allow this first (and sometimes the second) season to pass. Most bitches go into season twice per year. If you do plan to breed your Beagle in the future, then spaying is not an option to prevent unwanted offspring.

Pseudopregnancy (false pregnancy)

A false pregnancy is a not uncommon occurrence. The female behaves as if she has a litter. She takes all kinds of things to her nesting place and treats them like puppies. Her milk teats swell and sometimes milk is actually produced. The female will sometimes behave aggressively towards people or other animals, as if she is defending her young. False pregnancies usually begin two months after a season and can last a number of weeks. If it happens to a bitch once, it will often then occur after every season. If the condition repeats itself, spaying is the best solution, because continual false pregnancies increase the risk of womb or teat conditions.

Preparing to breed

If you do plan to breed a litter of puppies, you must first wait for your female to be physically and mentally full-grown. In any event you must let her first season pass. To mate a bitch, you need a male. You could simply let her out on the street and she will almost certainly quickly return home pregnant. But if you have a pure-bred Beagle, then it certainly makes sense to mate her with the best possible candidate, even if she does not have a pedigree. Proceed with caution and especially remember that accompanying a bitch through pregnancy, birth and the first eight to twelve weeks afterwards is a time consuming affair. Never breed a bitch that has congenital defects. The same goes for hyperactive, nervous and shy dogs. If your Beagle does have a pedigree, then mate her with a dog that also has one. For more information, contact the breed association.

Pregnancy

It's often difficult to tell at first when a bitch is pregnant. Only after about four weeks can you feel the pups in her abdomen. She will now slowly gain weight and her behavior will usually change. Her teats will swell during the last few weeks of pregnancy. The average pregnancy lasts 63 days, and

costs her a lot of energy. In the beginning she is fed her normal amount of food, but her nutritional needs increase greatly during the second half of the pregnancy. Give her approximately fifteen percent more food each week from the fifth week on. The mother-to-be needs extra energy and proteins during this phase of her pregnancy. During the last weeks you can give her a concentrated food, rich in energy, such as dry puppy food. Divide this into several small portions per day, because she can no longer deal with large portions of food. Towards the end of the pregnancy, her energy needs can easily be one-and-a-half times more than usual.

After about seven weeks the mother will start to demonstrate nesting behavior and starts to look for a place to give birth to her young. This might be her own basket or a special birthing box. This must be ready at least a week before the birth to give the mother time to get used to it. The basket or box should preferably be in a quiet place.

The birth

Most births take place 62 to 63 days after mating. The behavior of the female is usually an indication as to whether it still has time to go or whether the birth is imminent. Most

indications, such as the swelling of the teats and hair loss around them come at the same time. One may also notice the female's flanks retracting (pulling in of the pelvic muscles). Nest-building behavior such as hiding away, digging, scratching and turning in circles are the result of hormone changes. The mother-to-be is preparing the nest. One often also sees a change in facial expression. The most reliable indicator for an imminent birth is a drop in body temperature and the consequent trembling, which is sometimes mistaken for a sign of fear. A dog's normal temperature is 101-102.5°F. Twenty-four hours before the birth, it drops to 99°F, and then the birth process itself starts. Contractions become more intensive. As the amniotic sac is expelled, the bitch will lick around her vulva intensively, massaging the area and preventing it tearing during the birth. While pressing, the female will turn in circles around the nest and press against the side of the birthing pen to exert more power. The pups are born head or tail first. The latter, a so-called breech birth, usually takes longer than a head-first birth. There are pauses between each birth, and the young mother uses these pauses to lick her newly born puppies clean and to feed them. It goes without saying that it should be calm in the area around the mother during the birth. Don't allow strangers in and give her the feeling that she and you are going to deal with the matter together. It's up to you to make sure everything is calm and that there are no panic situations. Her behavior is to a large extent dependent on you; if you're calm, the mother will feel at peace and in good hands. An average litter is three to nine puppies. In most cases the birth will pass without problems. Of course, you must contact your veterinarian immediately if you suspect a problem!

It's a good idea to notify your veterinarian in advance when you are expecting a birth and agree arrangements with him or her.

Suckling

After birth, the mother starts to produce milk. The suckling period is very demanding. During the first three to four weeks the pups rely entirely on their mother's milk. During this time she needs extra food and fluids. This can be up to three or four times the normal amount. If she's producing too little milk, supplement the puppies with a milk-replacer. A veterinarian should be consulted if inadequagte milk production is suspected.

You can give the puppies some supplemental solid food when they are three to four weeks old. There are special puppy foods available that follow on well from the mother's milk and can easily be eaten with their milk teeth.

Ideally, the puppies are fully weaned at an age of six or seven weeks, i.e., they no longer drink their mother's milk. The mother's milk production gradually stops and her food needs also drop. Within a couple of weeks after weaning, the mother should again be getting the same amount of food as before the pregnancy.

Spaying and castration

If you do not plan to use your dog for breeding, neutering is recommended because of health benefits, population control, and the reduction of behavioral problems.

A female dog is spayed, and during this operation the uterus and the ovaries are removed. The bitch no longer goes into season and can never become pregnant. The best age for spaying is approximately six months, prior to the first heat cycle.

A male dog is castrated, and during this operation the testicles are removed. Castration can take place at any age but the best age is between 4 and 6 months.

Sports and shows

A Beagle is a real hunting dog that won't like to lie around. It will be a true companion with whom you can do almost anything if you do enough together.

This chapter offers just a brief look at some of the possibilities. The breed association will be happy to help you with more details.

Competitive events

The American Kennel Club competitve events fall into six categories: dog shows, obedience trials, tracking tests, field trials, hunting trials, and herding. Dog shows emphasize conformation, using the breed standard to compare one dog to another. Obedience trials test how well a dog can perform a series of prescribed exercises. Obedience is a competition of both handlers and dogs, and conformation has no bearing on the dog's ability to compete in obedience. Tracking tests require a dog to follow a trail by scent. Field trials are practical demonstrations of the dog's ability to perform. Hunting trials allow owners to receive evaluations of their dogs' hunting ability. Herding competitions involve leading a small group of livestock through a simple course. This information is courtesy the American Kennel Club.

Parasites

All dogs are vulnerable to various sorts of parasites. Parasites are tiny creatures that live at the expense of another animal. They feed on blood, skin and other body substances.

There are two main types. Internal parasites live within their host animal's body (tapeworms and roundworms) and external parasites live on the animals exterior, usually in its coat (fleas and ticks), but also in its ears (ear mites).

Fleas

Fleas feed on a dog's blood. They cause not only itching and skin problems, but can also carry infections such as tapeworm. In large numbers they can cause anemia and dogs can also become allergic to a flea's saliva, which can cause serious skin conditions. So it's important to treat dog for fleas as effectively as possible, not just on the dog itself but also in its surroundings. For treatment on the animal, there are various medications: drops for the neck and to put it in its food, flea collars, long-life sprays and flea powders. There are various sprays in pet stores that can be used to eradicate fleas in the dog's immediate surroundings. Choose a spray that kills both adult fleas and their larvae. If your dog rides in your car, you should spray that too. Fleas can also affect other pets, so you should treat those too. When spraying a room, cover any aquarium or fishbowl. If the spray reaches the water, it can be fatal for your fish!

Your veterinarian and pet store have a wide range of flea treatments and can advise you on the subject.

Ticks

Ticks are small, spider-like parasites. They feed on the blood of the animal or person they've settled on. A tick looks like a tiny, gray-colored leather bag with eight feet. When it has sucked itself full, it can easily be five to ten times its own size and is darker in color. Dogs usually fall victim to ticks in bushes, woods or long grass. Ticks cause not only irritation by their blood sucking but can also carry a number of serious diseases. Your veterinarian can prescribe a special preventative treatment if you live or are planning to take your dog to an infested region. It is important to fight ticks as effectively as possible.

Check your dog regularly, especially when its been running free in woods and bushes. Removing a tick is simple using a tweezer. Wear gloves and grip the tick with the tweezer, as close to the dog's skin as possible and carefully pull it out. Be sure the entire tick has been removed, especially the head, which has attached to the dog's skin. Wash your hands thoroughly after removing ticks. You must disinfect the spot where the tick had been using iodine to prevent infection. Never soak the tick in alcohol, ether, or oil. In a shock reaction the tick may discharge the infected contents of its stomach into the dog's skin.

Intestinal worms

Dogs can suffer from various types of intestinal worms, most commonly tapeworms and roundworms. Tapeworms can cause diarrhea and poor condition. With a tapeworm infection you can sometimes find small pieces of the worm (which look like grains of white rice) around the dog's anus or on its bed. In this case, the dog must be wormed. You should also check your dog for fleas, which carry the tapeworm infection. Roundworm infection is a condition that can recur regularly. Puppies are often infected by their mother at or before birth. Roundworms cause problems (particularly in younger dogs), such as diarrhea, loss of weight and stagnated growth. In serious cases the pup becomes thin, but with a swollen belly. It may vomit and you can then see the worms in its vomit. The worms, resembling spaghetti, may also appear in the feces. Puppies are checked for worms and given worming medications routinely as a part of regular veterinary care. Adult dogs should be tested for worms annually and treated as recommended by your veterinarian.

Heartworms

Heartworms are parasites spread by mosquitoes. Heartworm disease can be found in almost all parts of the U.S. with greatest incidence in areas with heavy mosquito populations. The adult heartworm lives in the heart and surrounding vessels of the dog and produces offspring, called microfilaria, which circulate in the blood of the infected animal. When a mosquito bites an infected pet, the microfilaria enter the mosquito and become infective larvae. They can then infect another pet bitten by that mosquito and grow into adult heartworms, resulting in heartworm disease.

Puppies are started on a preventative medication at the first visit to the veterinarian. These medications prevent the larvae from developing into adult heartworms. Annual or biannual screening tests are then recommended, even when dogs are on heartworm preventatives.Signs of canine heartworm disease include coughing, difficulty breathing, weight loss, poor hair coat, and fatigue. Prompt detection and early treatment of heartworm disease is important.

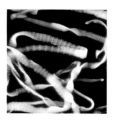

Tick

Tapeworms

Roundworms

Your Beagle's health

The space in this small book is too limited to go into the medical ups and downs of the German Shepherd.

Beagles are commonly used in research laboratories, so much is known about medical conditions in Beagles. Following are conditions that occur more commonly than others.

Hypothyroidism

This is a deficiency of thyroid hormones resulting in clinical signs involving almost all organ systems. Common clinical signs are rough and scaly skin, hair loss, and weight gain, though the list is much more extensive. Diagnosis is made by blood tests, and medication is available to treat the disease..

Heart disease

Two congenital (i.e., present at birth) heart diseases are common in Beagles: pulmonic stenoisis and ventricular septal defect (VSD). Both are diagnosed by a veterinarian through physical exam, radiographs and echocardiography. Treatment and prognosis vary according to severity of the defect(s).

Demodectic mange

Demodex cunis is a mite which, in small numbers, is present on normal canine skin. Deficiency of the dog's immune system can cause the mite to overpopulate the skin and cause severe skin conditions ranging from local areas of hair loss to generalized hair loss, scaling and secondary infection. Your veterinarian will provide you with treatment recommendations.

Distichiasis

This is a condition in which eyelashes grow abnormally on the margin of the eyelid, causing problems such as tearing, spasms of the eyelids, red conjunctiva, and corneal ulceration. Topical medications can help in mild cases, but surgery may be necessary for adequate treatment.

Ectopic cilia

This is a condition in which eyelashes grow on the inner surface (conjunctiva) of the eyelid. This can also cause the problems mentioned above. Treatment is the same.

Glaucoma

This is an increased pressure in the eye which, without treatment, can lead to pain and blindness. It usually occurs first in Beagles under the age of three years, so any abnormalities of the eye such as excessive discharge, pain, red/inflamed eyes or enlargement of the eye should be examined immediately by a veterinarian.

PRA (Progressive Retinal Atrophy)

PRA is a degeneration of the retina that inevitably leads to blindness at about five years of age. Dogs used for breeding should be checked for this condition annually.

Intervertebral Disc Disease

Intervertebral Disc Disease is a common problem seen in the

Beagle. It is characterized by a degeneration of discs throughout the spinal column. Acute disc ruptures can occur in either the neck or the back regions, resulting in different clinical signs and treatment approaches. Ruptures in the neck usually cause an acute onset of pain and can be treated medically or surgically. Disc ruptures in the back can result in rear limb weakness or paralysis and can be a surgical emergency. In either case, immediate veterinary attention should be sought.

Patellla Luxation

Patella (kneecap) luxation is a developmental disorder that may occur in some dogs. This is a condition characterized by intermittent non-weight-bearing rear limb lameness. The lameness results from a sudden dislocation of the kneecap out of the groove on the end of the thighbone. In many cases the kneecap will spontaneously return to the groove and the lameness immediately resolves. There are different grades of this disorder which in turn result in varying degrees of lameness. The condition often first appears in dogs after six months of age, but severe forms can appear in Beagles as young as four weeks of age. The luxation is surgically correctable, and owers should consider surgery if the lameness is both frequent and severe.

Preventative medicine

Regular veterinary examinations are essential for the health of all puppies and adult dogs. During these visits, your veterinarian will give your pet a complete physical examination and also recommend the appropriate vaccinations, heartworm medications, and flea and tick preventions. Your veterinarian can also help with

behavioral problems.

Immunization programs will vary from city to city, depending on local conditions. Your veterinarian can best recommend an appropriate vaccination schedule for puppies and adult dogs. Most puppies will receive first vaccinations at six weeks of age, followed by booster vaccinations every 3-4 weeks until 3-4 months of age. Adult dogs are usually vaccinated annually, depnding on individual circumstances. Vaccinations will most likely include distemper, adenovirus, parvovirus, and rabies. Other vaccines administered may include hepatitis, leptospirosis, parainfluenza, corona virus, bordetella, and Lyme disease, again, accorind to your veterinarian's protocol.

Beagle facts on the web

NATIONAL BEAGLE CLUB OF AMERICA
www.clubs.akc.org/NBC/index.htm
This is the official website of the National Beagle Club and contains a wealth of information about Beagles, breeders, shows, training and health care, and other important facts.

AMERICAN KENNEL CLUB
www.akc.org
The official website of the American Kennel Club great all-around site providing everything you need to know about breeds and finding the right dog and how to raise it.

AMERICAN VETERINARY MEDICAL ASSOCIATION
www.avma.org
The official website of the national association of veterinarians that has sever useful sits for dog owners regarding selection and care of dogs.

AMERICAN ANIMAL HEALTH ASSOCIATION
www.healthypet.com
The official website of the AAHA, an organization of 25,000 veterinary care providers committed to excellence in small animal care.

CYBERDOG
www.cyberpet.com/cyberdog
Contains down-to-earth information on dogs and dog care.

DOG BREED INFO CENTER
www.dogbreedinfo.com
An informative, easy to follow site designed to make choosing and living with a dog easy.

DOG NEWS
www.dognews.com
The official website of *Dog News The Digest of American Dogs*. An informative site containing news and information about not only purebred dogs, but all dogs.

INFODOG
www.infodog.com
A website containing listings of all the superintended dog shows in the United States and information on how to register your dog for shows.

MYPETSTOP.COM
www.mypetstop.com
A mutilingual website that offers dog care, breed, and behavior information, vet advice, breeder contacts

WALTHAM
www.waltham.com
WALTHAM is a leading authority in pet care and this site includes extensive information on all aspects of dog care, training, and nutrition.

Profile of the Beagle

Name:	Beagle
F.C.I.-classification:	Breed group:
	Scent hounds and related breeds
	(group VI)
F.C.I. Standard:	23/24 June 1987, Jerusalem
Origin:	England
Original tasks:	Hunting for small game
Shoulder height:	Male: 13 – 16 inches
	Female: 13 – 16 inches
Weight:	Male approx.: 25 – 35 lbs.
	Female approx.: 20 – 30 lbs.
Average life expectancy:	10-13 years